GUPPIES

By Spencer Glass

Of all the warm water fishes kept in the aquarium, none has been around so long nor has become so popular as the guppy. It exists in more varieties of color and form (mainly their fins) than any other fish and this includes the goldfish (which is not a warm water fish!). It is peaceful and usually can be kept with any other fish. The "usually" means that the "any other fish" will probably eat the guppy! So, because they are so small, hardly ever reaching two inches in body length (without the tail), so hardy and so beautiful, they deserve an aquarium of their own. This aquarium can contain lovely, delicate plants and other small fishes like cardinal tetras, but guppies really do best by themselves. Get a small guppy tank and see for yourself. A ten gallon aquarium will be fine.

Dr. Herbert R. Axelrod

What are YearBOOKs?

Because keeping Guppies as pets is growing at a rapid pace, information on their selection, care and breeding is vitally needed in the marketplace. Books, the usual way information of this sort is transmitted, can be too slow. Sometimes by the time a book is written and published, the material contained therein is a year or two old...and no new material has been added during that time. Only a book in a magazine form can bring breaking stories and current information. A magazine is streamlined in production, so we have adopted certain magazine publishing techniques in the creation of this yearBOOK. Magazines also can be much cheaper than books because they are supported by advertising. To combine these assets into a great publication, we issued this yearBOOK in both magazine and book format at different prices.

CONTENTS

Guppies 2
Fish-tory 4
Keeping Guppies 5
It's Guppy Time 14
Color Varieties & Patterns 18
Feeding 31
Breeding Your Guppies 38
Diseases 57

yearBOOK

yearBOOKS, INC.
Dr. Herbert R. Axelrod,
   Founder & Chairman
Neal Pronek
   Chief Editor

yearBOOKS are all photo composed, color separated, and designed on Scitex equipment in Neptune, N.J. with the following staff:

DIGITAL PRE-PRESS
   Robert Onyrscuk
   Jose Reyes
   Michael L. Secord

COMPUTER ART
   Sherise Buhagiar
   Patti Escabi
   Sandra Taylor Gale
   Pat Marotta
   Candida Moreira
   Joanne Muzyka

Advertising Sales
George Campbell
   Chief
Amy Manning
   Director

©yearBOOKS,Inc.
1 TFH Plaza
Neptune, N.J. 07753
Completely manufactured in Neptune, N.J. USA

GUPPIES

Look at this baby with its sleek lines and well appointed features... Moving from front to rear you can see that this model is well designed and aerodynamically styled. Now, while you see that these mechanical

addition to the wonderful proportions they lend, they are available in a vast array of colors. Even tail fin designs vary, depending on make and model selected.

Perhaps at this point I've confused you into believing you happened upon a 1964

to one of the most popular aquarium fish in the hobby almost from the advent of aquarium keeping in the United States. Of course you know we're talking about *Poecilia reticulata*, the good ol' guppy to you and me.

A flamingo double swordtail male guppy. Photo by Tanaka.

components are certainly a plus, it is the esthetically pleasing aspects that are drawing most consumers toward this wonderful work. Just gaze at the tail fins for a moment. In

edition of *Car and Driver*. You think you're about to read this book about aquarium fishes, and here the author is ranting on about a 1964 Cadillac.

Actually, I am referring

Almost all of us have kept guppies from one time or another. Why not? They are beautiful. Aside from their splendor, they are an interesting fish as well. Kids and adults alike seem to salivate over the prospect of having baby guppies arrive in our aquariums. You say they're livebearers, too! What's that mean? It means what it says, the guppy's young are born as living, breathing, swimming creatures. Yes, the majority of fish are egglayers. However, there is a select group of fish that internally fertilize and deliver free-swimming young at gestation. The most popular of this group of aquarium kept fishes are: swordtails, platies, mollies and, of course, guppies!

As you will soon discover, the guppy is a very hardy, interesting fish to keep and breed. They make for a very relaxing picture in your favorite sitting room as they swim peacefully back and forth through the mid-level in your aquarium.

Throughout the pages of this book, I will provide you with the necessary details to successfully keep guppies in your aquarium as well as general guidelines for breeding your guppies.

Nature did not give guppies these beautiful looks on her own. She merely gave them the genetic **potential.** Man did the rest.

You may choose to just let nature take its course, or you may choose to embark on your own research and development program of guppy propagation. Either way, your experience will more than likely be a pleasant one.

Metallic golden guppies are a very rare sight. These were bred and photographed by Kenjiro Tanaka, Osaka, Japan. Since most of the guppies used to illustrate this book came from Tanaka, readers who have questions may contact him by fax at (724) 23-7110. You must get the country code.

FISH-TORY

Actually, the guppy should have never been called a guppy at all. In scientific circles, newly discovered specimens of flora and fauna are given Latin name designations to specifically mark individual characteristics unique to the species. In years gone by, our global communications were nothing like what they are today. Often times, a newly discovered specimen

rules of nomenclature dictate it was subsequently branded with its Latin name, *Poecilia reticulata*. The year was 1859, so it was a long time ago.

Now Mr. Peters didn't have the use of fax machines, long distance phone service or e-mail for that matter. So, in the meantime there were other explorers picking up the same little fish of different

from Trinidad to be evaluated and described by the Ichthyology Department of the British Museum. British ichthyologist Dr. Albert Guenther mistakenly labelled this fish as a new discovery and subsequently named it after who he thought was its original discoverer...*Girardinus guppyi.*

For it was an English botanist who ultimately got

Two wild male guppies. This is the way they exist in nature. Photo by Tanaka.

was tagged with several designations. Such is the case with the guppy.

A German scientist, Wilhelm Peters, described a small fish discovered in Venezuela. As scientific

but similar color variations in Venezuelan waters. Each made his own scientific description. One such scientist, an English botanist to be exact, brought back some preserved fish

credit for discovering a fish that was already discovered. But the name stuck. So now for all eternity this pretty little fish will always bear the name **"guppy"** after Robert Guppy.

KEEPING GUPPIES

There is no great ancient Chinese secret you need to master in order to successfully keep guppies. However, some knowledge of basic water quality will help you a long way toward not only keeping them alive, but breeding them with a certain mastery as well.

Most of us take our initial water supply for our aquariums right out of the tap. Many of us acquire our water from municipally controlled supplies, while many make use of underground well water. There are also those of us who obtain water of the bottled variety for drinking purposes. Oddly enough, while all three may be clear fluids that look like water, feel like water, and taste like water, they may all have very differing compositions. They may vary in pH values, hardness factors, chlorine and other chemical levels. They may even include pollutants. How do these factors affect your guppies? That's what we'll address in this chapter.

Don't break out in a sweat either if you've never considered these factors before. Many fishkeepers never even stop to think that "pH balanced" isn't only a term for shampoos. Some may even think that

"hardness" has to do with how difficult it is to turn on the faucet. Now I may joke about these things, but actually these concepts are relatively simple. And a simple understanding of these is all you need to keep your guppies, and other fish as well, happy and healthy.

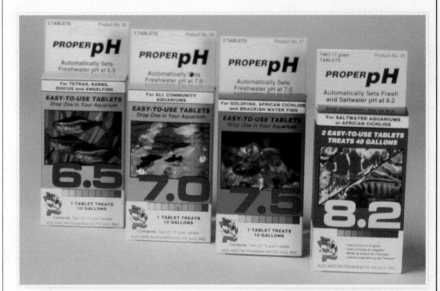

Products that set the pH to a predetermined level adjust the chemistry of the aquarium water to suit a particular species. Photo courtesy of Aquarium Pharmaceuticals.

pH

There are intricate definitions in scientific books as to exactly what pH is and does. For our purposes here, let us say the pH is a measure of acidity or alkalinity. A neutral pH level would be measured as 7.0 on the pH scale. This would mean the water is neither acidic nor alkaline. Lower values of the scale represent proportions of acidity. Small amounts of acidity would be represented by a pH value of 6.5. The lower on the scale you go the higher the amounts of acidity there are in the water. Conversely, the higher up on the pH scale you go, the higher the alkaline levels. Marine fish prefer pH levels in the 8.0 to 8.5 range. African cichlids emanating from the Rift Lakes also prefer their water on the higher end of the pH scale. What about guppies?

One great thing about guppies, they're quite resilient. Guppies will do just fine in water with pH levels from 6.4 to 7.5 with no signs of distress. Your job: Keep things steady. Know what the pH level is coming out of your tap. If it is to one extreme or the other (it should never be too acid, or there's a problem with your water supply), you can control and adjust it chemically. All aquarium stores sell very easy to use and inexpensive pH test kits. This kit should be a part of every fishkeeper's artillery.

HARDNESS

What is water hardness, and how does it affect guppies? Very simply, hardness is a measure of dissolved salts in the water, most specifically calcium and magnesium. Simple to use test kits to measure hardness are available in most pet stores. They measure hardness using an indication of parts per million (ppm) of hardness. Zero to eighty ppm of hardness would be indicative of soft water. Water considered very hard would show values of over 300 ppm. There are other more intricate means of measuring and evaluating water hardness, but for our purposes here, this should suffice.

Guppies do prefer soft water. What does *"prefer"* mean exactly? It means their colors will be brighter, their life span will be longer, they may eat better, be less prone to disease, and resultant broods will be larger and stronger. This is by no means a hard and fast rule. There will always be extraneous factors affecting these conditions. Guppies can and often will thrive in harder waters. Again, just watch out for extremes.

CHLORINE

Chlorine? Why would chlorine be in my water? They only put chlorine into pools. They don't put chlorine into your drinking water. Chlorine is a dangerous chemical...isn't it? It can be. More to fish than to you, however. Chlorine is put into swimming pools to prevent the build-up of dangerous bacteria. The same goes with your water supply, even more so during warmer weather when bacteria levels have a tendency to rise quickly. You should know that the amount of chlorine dumped into a swimming pool is significantly more than that put into the water supply.

Staying on the subject of

Green double swordtail male guppy. Photo by Tanaka.

pools, have you ever noticed there are times you come out of the pool with burning, bloodshot eyes? As your eyes and mucous membranes burn from too much chlorine, imagine what it does to a fish's delicate gill membranes. It burns, and it can burn bad. Too much chlorine can and will kill your fish. This is one reason why you don't want to set up your tank and put fish in it on the same day.

Luckily, this dilemma is easily solved. When adding water to your existing aquarium there are instant water de-chlorinators on the market.

Another option is to age the water. Let it sit exposed to the air. Chlorine gases will dissipate over a period of 24 hours and render it safe to use for your aquarium. Every fishkeeper would be well served to have one of those 5 gallon water cooler jugs available to set aside some water. You can get rid of the chlorine even more quickly by agitating the water, as with heavy aeration. Agitation, however, will not be effective in dissipating chloramine; it helps only with chlorine.

AMMONIA

Just as carbon monoxide can swiftly kill an exposed person, so too can the presence of ammonia in the aquarium kill your fish. Fish's waste products, especially urea, are actually ammonia by-products. Ammonia poisoning can

result in symptoms including increased respiration, reddened fins or gills, lethargy, lack of appetite, as well as others with the end result...death.

Low levels of pH (4.5 to 7.0 +/-) combined with ammonia are tolerable, though not recommended. High levels of pH (7.2 and up) combined with ammonia are highly toxic! If you for any reason whatsoever suspect

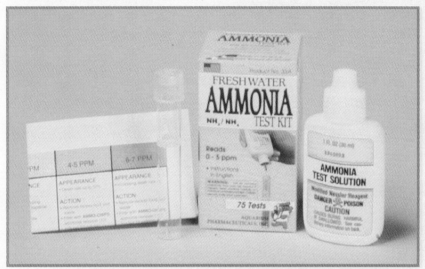

Test kits that enable the hobbyist to monitor various factors affecting the quality of the water, such as its ammonia content, are relatively inexpensive and easy to use. Photo courtesy of Aquarium Pharmaceuticals.

ammonia build up in your aquarium, immediately make a water test utilizing an ammonia test kit. Along with the pH test kit, the ammonia test kit should be part of every hobbyist's arsenal.

CONTROLLING AMMONIA

The first step in controlling and correcting excess (the slightest trace is considered excessive)

ammonia is understanding how it occurred in the first place. Proper filtration and regular tank maintenance are the keys to control. Even so there are other causal factors that can lead to a rise in ammonia levels.

There is a four-step process known as the *nitrogen cycle*. This process is initiated by the fish. The fish release their waste into the water. If filtration systems are working

correctly, you have microscopic bacteria *(Nitrosomonas)* living in the water that break the ammonia down into a less toxic substance known as *nitrite*.

After the *Nitrosomonas* do their job, bacteria of the genus *Nitrobacter* break the nitrites down to less toxic substances. These are known as *nitrates*. Low levels of nitrates are generally harmless to freshwater fish.

You complete the cycle by diluting any remaining nitrates with a partial water change. Opinions vary on the volume and frequency of these water changes. I can confidently say that more frequent less voluminous water changes are best. For example, changing 10% to 20% of the volume weekly would be graciously welcomed by many fish. Your schedule or desire may not be so accommodating, and that is what is great about fish. They're so understanding.

When giving advice to novice fish keepers I always try to stay in the middle mixing necessity with reality. Therefore, a 20% to 25% bi-weekly water change is quite sufficient. Can you go longer than that? Welllllllll...yes, maybe. Many hobbyists make their water changes on a monthly basis. When they do, they usually change about 33% of the water.

Actually, going one month should be reserved for more experienced aquarists, and they rarely go past the one month mark. At that point you are seriously risking ammonia poisoning. But what do you do if you discover that your tank is full of ammonia? How do you save your fish? Simple, but act quickly, meaning now! Immediately change 33% to 50% of your water with a water siphon, vacuuming the gravel bed as you go. Suspend feeding for 24 hours.

For most fishes including guppies, it is prudent (if you haven't already) to add a teaspoon of aquarium salt per gallon of water. You should see your fish responding positively within the day.

The *Nitrosomonas* and *Nitrobacter* bacteria need a place to live and grow in order to do their job. This place of residence is usually within the filtration system. The undergravel filter (UGF) is an excellent home for them. Air is pumped through the UGF and oxygenates the gravel bed. The oxygenated gravel serves as an incredible surface area on which these bacteria can reside and colonize. This is a very good form of filtration to promote good bacterial growth in the aquarium.

A secondary form of filtration that works in

The eye-spot guppy features a large black spot surrounded by a halo. All the dots on the body are outlined by highlights. Photo by Tanaka.

These swordtail guppies feature very thick double swords (upper and lower rays of the tail) plus large black spots on the caudal peduncle. Photo by Tanaka.

promoting bacterial growth, but not quite as well, is the power filter. Generally this is a device that hangs on the back of the tank and draws water through a series of filtration media (foam and carbon) and drops it back into the aquarium. Bacteria will live on these filtration media. Unbeknownst to many an aquarium keeper, when they change the filtration material they throw away most of the bacteria. Here's a little hint. Before chucking that yucky filter stuff, let it drip onto the new stuff. This will keep things going. The use of both devices (undergravel filter and power filter) in tandem is the optimum method of employing filtration in your tank.

There are other forms of filtration available on the market, but so far as guppies go, an undergravel filter combined with a small power filter will be more than ample.

There are several items that can cause an otherwise stable aquarium to suddenly be hit with a sharp increase in ammonia. We already talked about the accumulation of waste products. This can be avoided by doing partial water changes. Overfeeding and the accumulation of uneaten leftovers can certainly trigger an ammonia spike (sudden rise). Another cause could be the introduction of too many fish at the same time.

After the first month or so, the bacteria in your tank have attained a certain equilibrium. They maintain themselves in such numbers as to be able to break down the waste that is being delivered. If an inordinate waste load is suddenly added via extra fish, these bacteria will not have had sufficient time to build up to do their job. Both overfeeding and tank capacity will be dealt with later on in this book.

Of course you may find all of this knowledge a tad overwhelming, but don't let it get your goat. You'll get it down. Seriously, ammonia control is very easy. With normal routine maintenance and an eye for never overdoing it, ammonia will become a topic of the past.

SALT IN THE AQUARIUM
Many freshwater fish,

guppies included, come from rivers and streams that have a natural salt content. Not nearly as dense as marine water, but with a minimal content nonetheless.

Nature built such fishes to benefit from this salt content by making their breathing apparatus more functional with the salt content. Oxygen passes through the gills more easily in the presence of these dissolved salts. Without it they can and will survive. With it they will thrive.

The moral to this story: One teaspoon of salt per gallon of water is the best preventative medicine for guppies as well as many other fishes.

Note: When water evaporates the salt does not. When making a partial water change, add only enough salt for the volume of water removed.

Do not use table salt. Many table salts add anti-caking agents that are not good for your fish. It is best to buy an aquarium salt designed especially for that purpose.

THE GUPPY COMMUNITY

The most disappointing thing many new guppy owners find out is that not only do they find them beautiful, but so do their tankmates. So pretty are they, they are constantly harassed by the likes of tiger barbs, swordtails, mollies, angelfish, etc., etc., etc. Some of these so-called tankmates will stop at nothing for a bite of the luscious guppy tail. Why is this?

While the guppy is certainly a hardy fish, its grandiose tail makes it not one of the fastest swimmers in the tank. To add insult to injury, the flag-like appendage is a target for the other fishes in the tank. It may as well say, "Come get me." And they do. What inevitably happens is you end up with a tailless ratty-looking guppy that will end up with a subsequent bacterial or fungal infection. In that situation, the tail will never return to its normal state. Even if kept alone, the fish will never be the same.

What type of fish can you keep with guppies that won't ravage them? I have good news and bad news.

Okay, the bad news first. Not many. Even seemingly peaceful fish will be attracted to the guppy's tail. This would include most tetras, barbs, danios and the like that are swift swimmers. Even fish you

Blue golden double swordtail male guppy. Photo by Tanaka.

Tanaka's black guppies are a favorite in Japan; they have unique tails. Photo by Tanaka.

feel you don't see free swimming like eels, loaches, and pleco cats will come out in the evening to munch on your guppy's tail. One particular group of catfish known as corydoras can be kept with guppies. They are relatively slow, peaceful co-habitants that should not bother your guppies. Aside from being the perfect tankmates, the corydoras cats do a respectable job of picking up leftovers in the aquarium.

The good news is...what's so bad about keeping a tank of just guppies? Aargh! You gasp. A tank of only one kind of fish. Who keeps a tank full of one kind of fish? Actually many aquarists do just that. There's absolutely nothing wrong with studying a particular species of fish, and what better way of

doing that but by specifically focusing on that species. A tank full of guppies, large or small, with no one else to harass them, is a very beautiful sight.

Now that you've decided you're going to devote your tank to guppies only, just how many guppies can you squish into one tank? The same old rule you've probably already heard still applies. *"An inch of fish per gallon of water."* You can rest assured that following this rule will keep you safe from avoiding an ammonia spike caused by overcrowding.

There are ways to increase your tank capacity. If you are a beginner it is better to stay with the inch of fish per gallon rule. If you're a little more experienced you can add approximately 50%

more fish by following a few basic concepts that you've been employing already. Let's take a look at some.

1. Filtration: combining an undergravel filter along with a power filter is a necessity. It would further help your UGF by employing a powerhead rather than an air pump to power it.

2. Water changes: You once-a-monthers, forget it. To exceed your tank's normal capacity you want to do a 20% bi-weekly water change minimum.

3. Tankmates: Whether you have one or twenty guppies in your tank, combining them with unsuitable tankmates will lead to inevitable stress. Imagine someone chasing you around a room 24 hours a day. In a week you'd have a heart attack. So too your

TANK SIZE	DIMENSIONS	SURFACE AREA (square inches)
10 Gallons	10" x 20"	200
20 Gallon High	12" x 24"	288
20 Gallon Long	12" x 30"	360

guppies. The less stress on your fish the more likely they are to thrive with additional compatible roommates.

4. Overfeeding: This is probably the primary fishkeeper's sin. We tend to overfeed ourselves, so too we do it to our fish. In the wilds of nature a fish is on the ever constant search for whatever food source would be available. Rarely do they come upon an unending feast such as we provide them with in aquaria. Unfortunately, the fish can only take in only so much during one feeding. The excess tends to sink to the bottom, where it decays and fouls the aquarium. At the next feeding we do the same thing, and the next day the same, and the next day, and so on.

What you end up with is fish food soup. Just ladle it out of the aquarium and serve! What you really have going is decaying food depleting the oxygen content of the aquarium and causing a possible ammonia spike at the same time. This is certainly *not* a tank capable of housing several *extra* fish. When feeding, err on the side of underfeeding. Nature does. Frequent smaller meals are better than one large meal. A fish constantly

on the look-out for food is a fish with a healthy metabolism that will thrive when *properly* fed.

Take a look at the chapter on feeding to get a better idea of what to feed your guppies and how much.

5. Surface Area: Simply stated, the surface area of your tank would be the length x width of the top surface of your aquarium.

The important thing to know about surface area is that it is where oxygen is exchanged. The breaking of the surface area (by filtration or other means) allows the

Flamingo golden double swordtail with a very rarely seen red dorsal fin. Photo by Tanaka.

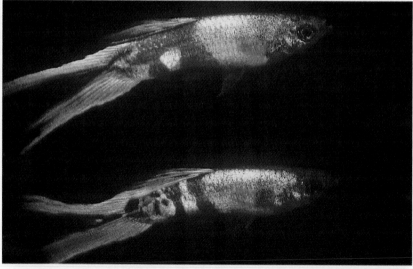

The convict double swordtail guppy. Photo by Tanaka.

oxygen to saturate the tank. As you can see by the graph that while a 20 gallon high tank has double the volume of a 10 gallon tank, the difference in surface area between the two is slightly over 40%.

Looking at the difference between the two types of 20 gallon tanks you will see that while they are both the same in volume, the 20 gallon long has 25% more surface area. The greater the surface area of the tank, the more oxygen that is able to be exchanged. Obviously the shorter longer tanks have a greater surface area than the higher shorter ones, hence these style tanks are more suited to house additional fish over the one inch per gallon rule.

Let's say you follow all of these guidelines, exactly how many fish can you put into your tank? This is a speculative question, however you can safely exceed the one inch per gallon rule. The larger the tank the more volume you have to displace the excess waste load the additional fish are going to place on the filtration system.

A ten gallon tank may safely accept an additional 30% more fish over the 10 inches giving you 13 inches of fish in your ten gallon tank. A 20 gallon high could house 30% more, too, while you could go with 40% more with the 20 gallon long variety, with its increased surface area.

This is a really nice guppy. Unfortunately it has been kept under the incorrect light. Guppies require special lamps to bring out the full range of their rainbow-like colors. Photo by Hans Joachim Richter.

While I keep many tanks to study various species of fish, I still keep my original 29 gallon tank as my community display tank. By following the aforementioned guidelines, I have increased my fish load from the original 29 inches to 45 inches. That's a 50% increase. I never have a problem.

You could do this too. I've never done it, but I really think a 29 gallon tank full of guppies would look absolutely spectacular. There's one final important item to keep in mind. Don't try to stock your tank to its maximum capacity all at once. Don't even try to do it quickly. The most successful way of accomplishing this feat is slooooooooooowly. Start with a few, adding more gradually over a period of months or even a year. I always try to keep a little extra room in my tank so when I come upon that irresistible specimen, I know I have room for it. We all

Your pet shop has lamps for every occasion as evidenced by this Aquarium Bulb Center. Photo courtesy of Penn Plax.

know, half the fun of keeping fish is shopping for them.

IT'S GUPPY TIME

Through selective, and sometimes not so selective, breeding the common guppy most often sold as a feeder fish, has evolved into a highly sought after creature. There are a myriad of varieties when it comes to guppies. Not only can you find them sporting such colors as red, green, blue, white, black, and yellow, but in combinations thereof as well.

Combine their beautiful colors with the variety of elegant tail shapes and you truly have a living gem. Many a guppy breeder has worked arduously to promote a certain strain of color or tail shape or both. One of the premier guppyholics was a man named Paul Hahnel. In the late 1930's Mr. Hahnel came to the United States.

> "Beautiful guppies don't just happen...they are cultivated. They come in many varieties, including different colors and finnage shapes. There is no great problem involved in breeding guppies if you are willing to give it the time and effort...and have patience. You don't need a great knowledge of genetics. You just need good eyes."
> —Dr. Herbert R. Axelrod

He got some of the wild guppies most often seen on the market at that time and nurtured them into the gorgeous fish we take for granted today.

Mr. Hahnel treated his guppies as if they were his children, with tender lovin' care. He performed copious water changes (not a familiar concept in the 1930's) and fed them better than most people who were keeping goldfish at the time. We talked about water changes in a previous chapter, and we'll deal with "feeding" in an upcoming section.

"I don't care what guppy you start with; give me any guppies. Just feed them good live foods and dried foods when you pass them from the left, and siphon off 10% of their water when you pass them from the right. Replace the water with aged good water. Throw away the bad males and just keep the good males. In a few years you'll have beautiful guppies." - Paul Hahnel, The Father of the Fancy Guppy.

This artistic double exposure, made in 1955 by Dr. Herbert R. Axelrod, portrays the legendary Paul Hahnel. Hahnel was a master cabinet maker who dabbled in guppies. Dr. Axelrod still uses the desk Hahnel made for him in 1957.

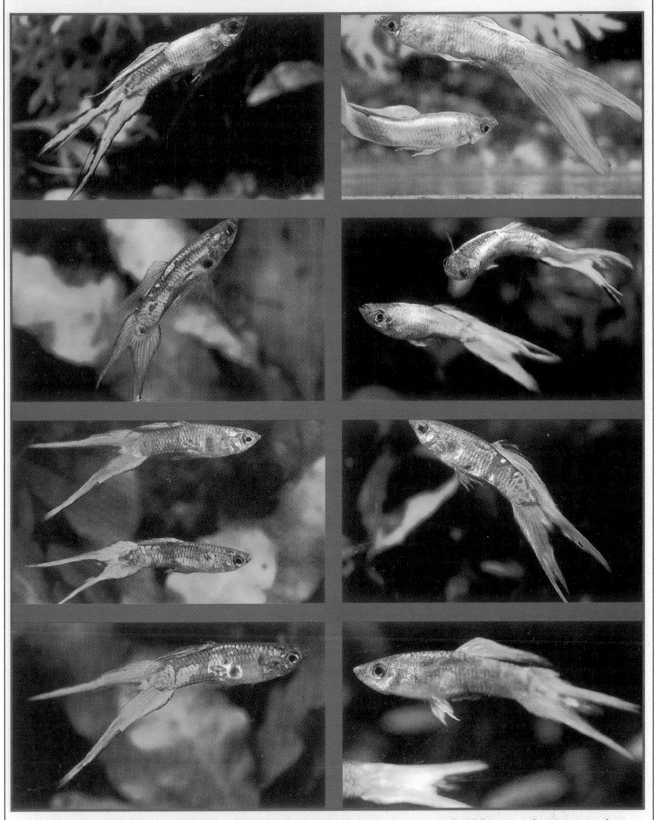

Various double swordtail guppies developed and photographed by Tanaka. Most of Tanaka's photos are dark because only with this dark contrast can the subtle colors of the male guppies be appreciated. Guppies kept in bright light always appear washed out.

And that's exactly what Paul Hahnel did, developing his very own strain: the Hahnel guppy. If you take a look at some of the more wild-like guppies (usually sold as feeders), then compare them with the guppies sold as "fancy," you can see how Mr. Hahnel really put some energy into his work.

The Hahnel guppy is not unlike many of the guppies seen for sale in the aquarium trade today. He selected the largest, most vividly colored males, and bred them to the largest, most brilliantly colored females. It doesn't take a brain surgeon to figure out the resultant progeny's proclivity. Of course, they weren't all show quality. Years of cultivating the positive attributes of the offspring led to bigger, brighter and better guppies. You can do the same, and we'll talk about breeding a little later on.

Over the years, as color and size were being tested and perfected, guppy breeders started experimenting with other bodily mutations, tail shape being the most popular with which to work.

TAIL TYPES

There are numerous tail types being bred and sold around the world. The International Fancy Guppy Association (IFGA; more on them later) has over 70 classes of guppies featuring a vast array of colors and tail types. The popularity of different tail shapes varies from country to country. In the United States and Canada, for example, the veiltails and deltatails are the most popular tail shapes, with relatively little attention paid to some of the tail shapes that are popular at British and Continental shows. Keep in mind that judging standards and nomenclature change from time to time and very definitely from country to country as regards both tail types and recognized colors.

This is a magnificent development in the eye-spot guppy with double tail highly decorated against a deep red basic color. Photo and fish by Tanaka.

Deltatail guppies in red, blue, purple and black depending upon how you see it! These are the popular guppies bred in Singapore and shipped worldwide. The fish shown here are probably American bred.

COLOR VARIETIES & PATTERNS

"Variety is the spice of life." If this little saying is true, then guppies offer an entire cabinet to the tropical fish hobbyist. Just take a look at some of the photos in this book. Even the mass bred plain-ol' feeder guppies show hints of miscellaneous colors. You can see hints of blue and red and black and green and orange, just to name several colors. It is from these little guys that

albino guppy is not truly devoid of color. As in all true albinos, the iris of the eye is red.

PINK FLAMINGO

The pink flamingo guppy is very similar in appearance to the albino guppy. It is, however, not an albino. The pink flamingo has pigmentation. This is characterized by the black in the eyes as well as the black variegation in the

SOLIDS

It is hard to find guppies with true solid coloration throughout their entire

A half-black body and white deltatail male guppy. Bred by Paul Evans; photo by Stan Shubel.

body such as the case with bettas. Instead what you will find is a fish that has a body and tail color that is predominantly the same. Often you will find that

Pink flamingo double swordtail male guppy. Fish and photo by Tanaka.

The intense color of this half-black deltatail was on display in Europe. Photo by Aqua press, MP&C Piednoir.

the truly gorgeous colors were derived and fixed.

ALBINO

The albino is a color form (or lack thereof) that is either loved or hated. An

tail. Further augmenting this guppy's features is a nice flowing delta tail.

The pink flamingo, with its stunning red features on a cream body, is a very pleasant looking fish.

solids will still have scales outlined in black while the fish's hue shines through. The tail is generally more solid than the body, though

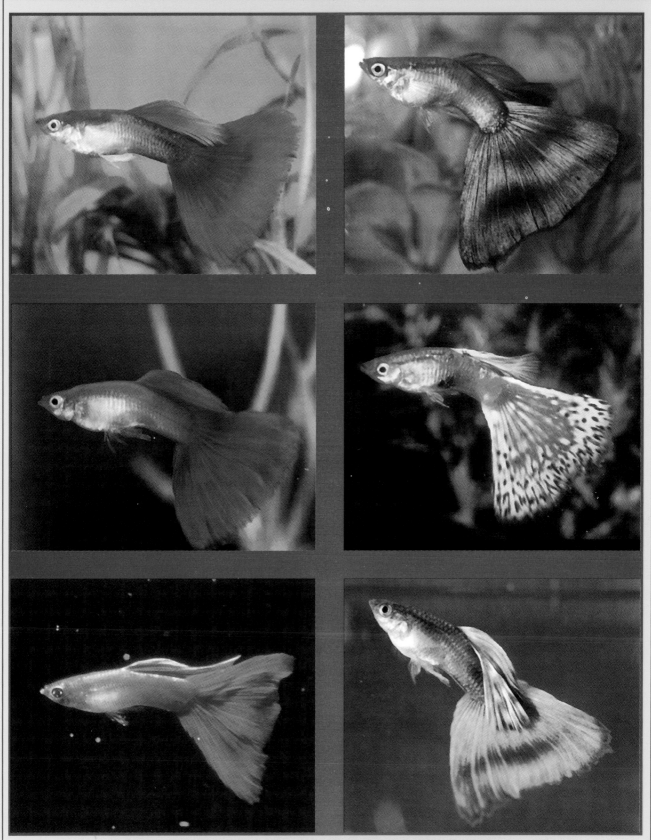

Modern deltatail guppies shown in red, white and blues.

One of the most interesting strains of guppy comes from Russia. The breeder and photographer H. Kyselov proudly presented this cross between a lacetail and a snakeskin with a huge deltatail.

The Tanaka lacetail has a distinct pattern of lace in its tail but it also has the snakeskin pattern on its body. Photo by Tanaka.

it can have strands of black or another color.

Solid colorations can include: blue, black, yellow, red, and most stunning, the green.

HALF-COLORS

Essentially a half-color is a guppy that has two separate colors; the tail is one color while the body is another. Actually, however, this is not completely true. The half-colors you see often have a tail that is of one solid coloration while the body is of mixed coloration of which one color is predominant. Additionally, you will see that in the half-colors the dorsal fin will be solid and the same

These are lovely Tanaka lace/snakeskins. Look at it as though their tails are spots circled with gold. Photo by Tanaka.

The Russian deltatail after a few generations of selective breeding by Tanaka. Photo by Tanaka.

color as the tail fin.

ENGLISH LACE

An English lace guppy is usually a guppy with a solid colored body with a symmetrical dotted pattern through the tail. More often than not, the English lace guppy is of the blue variety. Its body is usually black or dark blue, maybe even white or white with a blue hue, while the tail is variegated (having discrete markings of different

Opposite page: Russian deltatail snakeskin guppies. Photographed in Moscow, Russia by H. Kyselov.

colors) with speckles of orange, blue and/or white.

SNAKESKIN

Why they refer to this type of guppy as a snakeskin, I haven't figured out yet. While it does have a distinct body pattern, which snake it mimics is still a mystery. Nevertheless this guppy type is one of extreme popularity in the hobby.

There are various color forms available in the snakeskin guppy. The most prevalent are the yellow, red, blue, and green. For some reason I find all of the guppies of the green variety

the most pleasing. Unlike the English lace variety the markings on the tail of a snakeskin are completely asymmetrical. So too, with the body. You will often find in the snakeskins that there are traces of red and silver throughout the body. The markings, though, are not random, appearing as irregular blotches or spots as with many of the wild varieties of guppies. Moreso, you have an almost psychedelic pattern weaving its way across the fish's body. This pattern can be present on the fish's

Forty years ago, Paul Hahel and and Dr. Leon F. Whitney wrote the first comprehensive book about guppies. They established, for the first time, nomenclature for guppy tail shapes. These guppies were drawn from live specimens supplied by Hahnel, from the book *All about Guppies*.

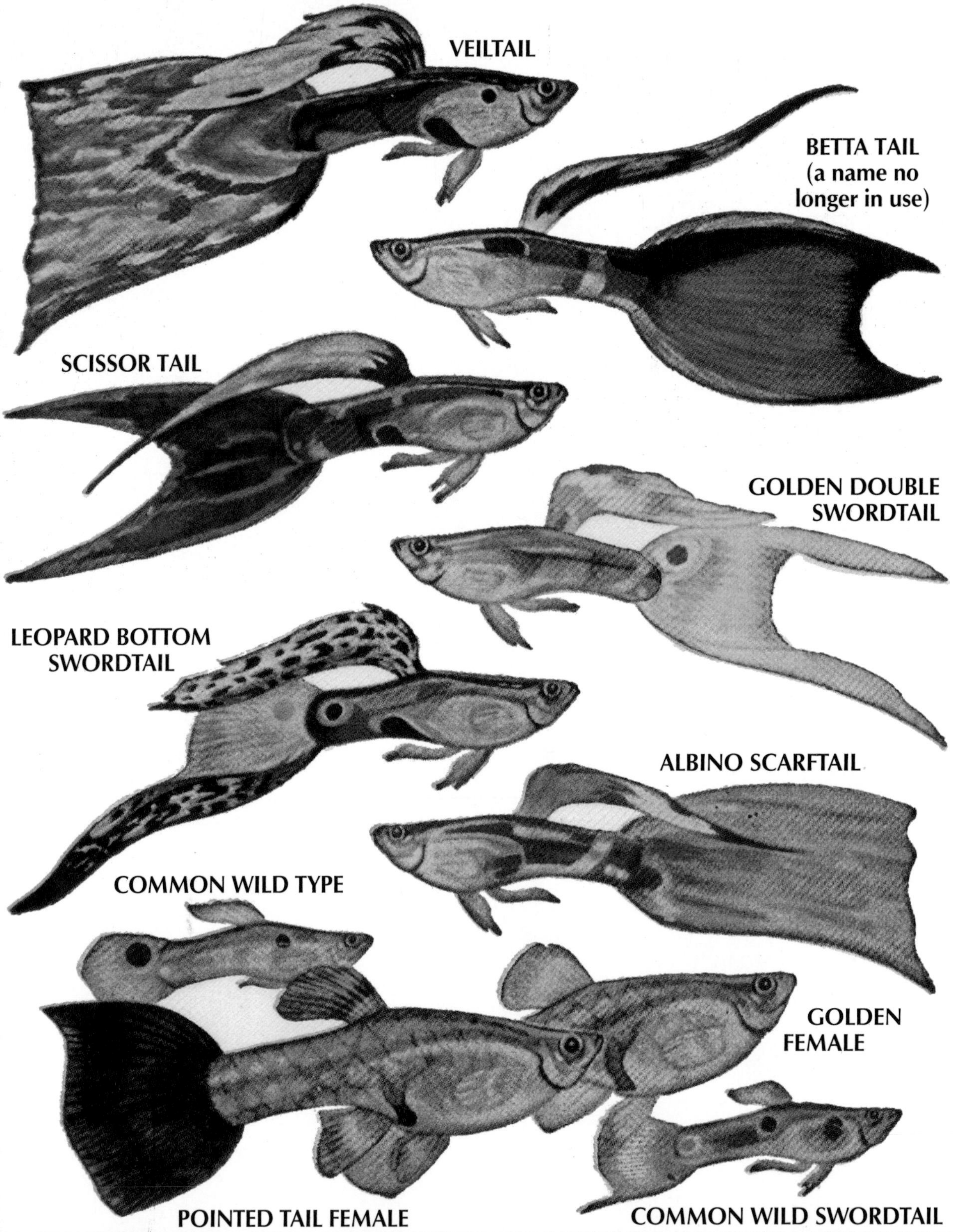

VEILTAIL

BETTA TAIL
(a name no
longer in use)

SCISSOR TAIL

GOLDEN DOUBLE
SWORDTAIL

LEOPARD BOTTOM
SWORDTAIL

ALBINO SCARFTAIL

COMMON WILD TYPE

GOLDEN
FEMALE

POINTED TAIL FEMALE

COMMON WILD SWORDTAIL

Guppies, like some other fishes, especially Discus, are given fancy names by their originators to differentiate them from competitive fish. The two fishes shown above and below are Spanish Dancers produced in Singapore by the Gan Aquarium Fish Farm. In Singapore these fishes are called *Pink Delicate Variegated Guppies*.

body along with a solid tail. Otherwise the pattern can proliferate itself throughout the entire body.

JADEHEAD

As it might sound the jadehead is a guppy variety with a jade-colored (dark green) head. The posterior of the jadehead is black through to the base of the caudal (tail) fin. The tail fin is green with a snakeskin pattern. Proper breeding of a jadehead can turn out quite a majestic looking fish.

GREEN COBRA

Obviously this is going to

Russian golden snakeskin guppies. Phot by H. Kyselov.

be a green guppy. A good Green Cobra will have an emerald green body and a tail that is variegated with a yellow tint.

SPANISH DANCER

Also referred to as a Spanish skirt, this variety of guppy is particularly distinguished by its tail. While the body color is somewhat nondescript, the tail can be said to be similar to the flashy Spanish dresses worn by flamenco dancers. In semi-circles of alternating strips of orange and blue, the tail of the Spanish dancer highlights itself among any other guppy variety.

This variegated guppy has an interesting tail. Its uniform body stripes and half eye-spot and snakeskin tail, slightly bifurcated, makes it a unique strain. Fish and photo by Tanaka.

VARIEGATED GUPPY

This term could be relegated to almost any guppy not falling into any particular category. Giving the vast differentiations possible within the guppy, it is certainly possible to throw an oddball out there. When this oddball guppy has its traits fixed via subsequent propagation it then earns itself a specific name designation.

This unique variegated guppy has no stripes on its body. It shows a few eye-spots. Photo and fish Tanaka.

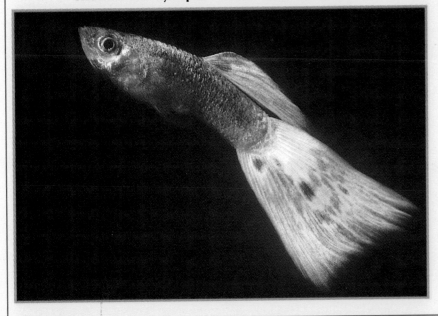

WHAT'S NEW!

The I.F.G.A. recognizes a number of classes for showing purposes that set various colors and tail types apart from one another. Any guppy produced will fall into a category referred to as Any Other Color, or AOC. While many of the guppies shown tend to be redundant year after year, there are several specimens shown in the AOC category that spark some interest.

A couple of the most recent inclusions would be a snakeskin guppy sporting horizontal or vertical bars through the body. This may not be totally eye-appealing, however it is different. Another entry was a 3/4 black guppy with black tail and black dorsal. The unusual feature of this

Paul Hahnel (left) with Stan Shubel in the 1960's.

guppy: a white dot on the dorsal fin.

One group once placed in the AOC group has now been given a specific class unto itself. This group would be the Pastels. The pastel group would include guppies with light coloration: pale blues, pale greens, pale yellow or golden. These may also include white coloration as well. One guppy considered stunning by some would be the all-white pastel guppy. Who knows what's next on the drawing board.

If you are interested in becoming a member of the I.F.G.A. you can write to them for information c/o: A.M. Mail Plus, 16651 Parthenia Street, North Hills, California 91343

Additional information on showing, keeping, and

THE PROPER CARE OF GUPPIES
by Stan Shubel, is considered the most modern, up-to-date book available on guppies.

breeding may also be gleaned from many of the books put out by T.F.H. Publications. One book specifically recommended is *The Proper Care of Guppies*, by guppy enthusiast Stan Shubel.

I have to admit, in writing this book I myself have learned a lot more about the "simple" guppy than I had expected. I bet you have too. The guppy is an endearing creature to young and old alike. You can have a lot of fun with them. You now know you don't need to be an expert to breed them. So don't be intimidated. And if your kids are spending too much time in front of the T.V. or video games just see what a tankful of guppies will do to change their interest.

Good luck. Have fun.

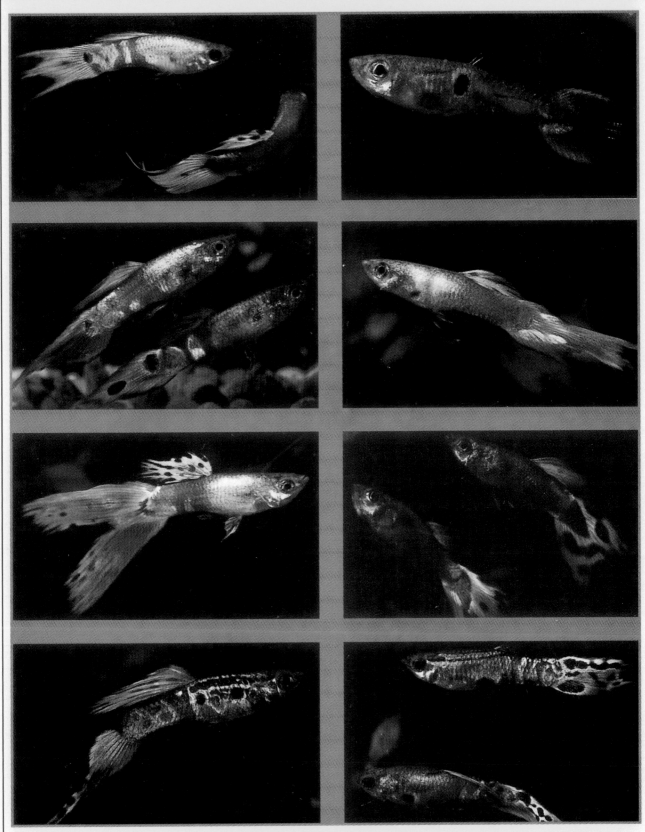

What do all of these Tanaka guppies have in commmon? They all have different tails, different color patterns, but each has a tell-tale eye-spot. Photos by Tanaka.

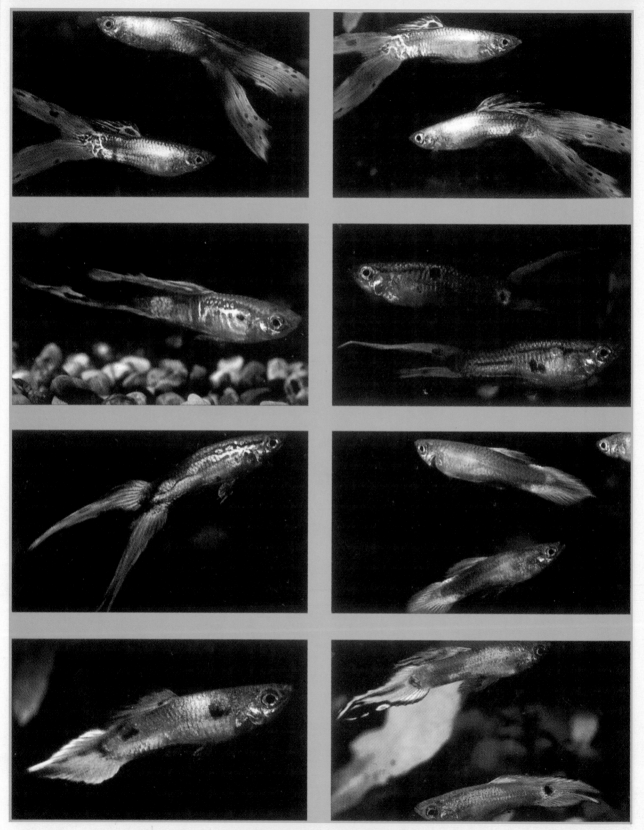

From the common to the semi-spectacular... more Tanaka guppies in a variety of tail shapes and colors. Photos by Tanaka.

FEEDING

One of the major downfalls of beginning aquarium keepers is their lack of knowledge with regard to feeding their fish. The same will evidently hold true for new guppy keepers. It is apparent that thousands of hobbyists successfully keep guppies as well as other sorts of tropical fish *sans* a degree in ichthyological nutrition. So it is true for you. What you do want to keep in mind, however, is the fact that in order for your fish to *thrive,* you need to take certain measures to assure their health. I always use the following analogy.

Could a person eat at a fast food joint every day and live? The answer is yes. But at what level of health? Usually a person with a poor diet, high in fat and excessive protein, will eventually falter. They will succumb to colds, viruses and flus more frequently than a person who maintains a diet more consistent with the four main food groups. Other residual symptoms may also develop as a result of a nutritional deficiency. The same holds true for fish.

Sure, you can go out and buy a giant tub of no brand flake food for several dollars that will seemingly last a lifetime. Your guppies will eat it, too. One problem, though. This "el cheapo" food is cheap for a reason. It is probably much lower in quality protein and other necessary nutritional content than the nationally advertised and better

At the huge Aquarama Fish Shows held in Singapore, the Gan Aquarium Fish Farm won Best Guppy with these green guppies. Unfortunately the lighting was bad, but the fish glistens in emerald green, even the tail.

known flake foods. We all know...you get what you pay for. Don't be penny-wise and pound foolish. Spend a little more. Your guppies will thank you.

They will thank you by showing off their colors more vibrantly. (That's what attracted you in the first place, isn't it?) They will swim through your aquarium with more exuberance. They will not need to eat as much to obtain equal nutritional

requirements, hence they will foul your water less. Spawning success will be greater, and subsequent fry (babies) will be more durable, ensuring you of a

Foods specifically formulated with the nutritional needs of guppies in mind come in a number of different forms and are widely available. Photo courtesy of Hikari.

larger throw. This is a big difference. Don't limit your feeding to only flake food.

I know. You just talked yourself into spending a couple extra bucks on the better flake food, and now I'm telling you to expand the diet even further. How'd you like to eat chicken every day for the rest of your life? Pretty boring, huh. Unless you're on a low cholesterol diet, you find that variety adds a little dimension to meal time. Fish are the same way. There are a lot of prepared foods available for your fish, and you would do them well to stock various kinds in your fish pantry.

The flake foods, of which there are many brands and varieties, are popular and easy to use. Some are intended for use specifically with guppies, and others are for general feeding purposes. Some are made of a wide range of substances, while others are based primarily on one basic ingredient.

Then there are the freeze-dried foods. These are (were) living organisms, flash frozen and packaged for feeding to your tropical fish. Freeze dried foods your guppies will relish include: tubifex worms, bloodworms, daphnia (water fleas) and mosquito larvae. Those of you with weak stomachs for insects will be glad to know you can satiate your fish's yearning for these items with a minimal amount of stomach discomfort on your part.

Next, let's take a walk down the frozen food aisle.

The most popular and eagerly accepted frozen food would be brine shrimp. Most of these foods are packed in flat bars and are kept in your freezer. You can break a piece off and throw it right into the tank. It will dissolve in front of your eyes as you watch your fish nip at it with an enthusiastic zeal.

These foods are also available in individual blister packs (compartmentalized ice cube tray-like forms) that make feeding as simple as "pop-em out" and "watch-em eat." A more economical way of simplifying frozen food feeding is to slice it yourself. Simply let the frozen slab thaw for about fifteen minutes. Take a sharp knife and slice the food up into little cubes, whatever size you like. When you're ready to feed, simply pull out a frozen

Flake foods are a convenient and popular means of feeding your guppy. They offer a wide range of foods and a very large range of package sizes. Photo courtesy of Hagen.

The Tanaka line of golden guppies. They are bred in various tail shapes. Photo by Tanaka.

food cube and drop it into the tank.

Frozen foods come in a wide variety, especially with the advent of specialized salt water fish frozen foods. For simplicity's sake you can be pretty safe using the frozen brine shrimp and/or the frozen bloodworms.

Two wild males collected in Trinidad. Photo and fish from Dr. Herbert R. Axelrod.

These will satisfy both your fish's appetite as well as nutritional requirements when balanced out with a flake food diet.

Other frozen foods available that your guppies would appreciate include: glassworms, daphnia, mosquito larvae, beef heart and others. It's not necessary to have every one, but try to keep at least, a couple different food items on hand.

Last, but certainly not least are the live foods. Live foods...egad! How could they eat live foods...that's...why that's uncivilized. Come on, get a grip. There's a food chain you know. Fish eat bugs, birds eat fish, mammals eat birds...you know. All kidding aside, there's nothing more nutritious, and nothing that will get your fish into better breeding condition than a regular dose of live foods. What kind of live foods, though?

The least expensive form of live foods you can feed to your guppies are the kind you can round up yourself. The easiest source would be your common everyday earthworm. The only problem is that there is no guppy out there that has the ability to suck down even a smallish earthworm. You're stuck chopping them up into tiny bit size morsels. This is not for the faint of heart. You literally have to take a worm, put it on the cutting board, and chop away.

You can visit your local lake and collect some mosquito larvae. This is a favorite food for all fish. Just make sure your fish

eat them **all** up or you may have some unwelcome guests in your home.

The easiest way to get live food for your fish is to buy it at your local aquarium store. Generally, they are pre-packaged for your convenience and sit on ice to suspend metamorphosis. Once you bring them home you can empty them into a plastic container with a lid or keep them in the refrigerator to serve the same purpose.

There are a number of these critters available for you to feed your guppies. Bloodworms, glassworms, blackworms, and tubifex worms are the most often seen live foods offered for sale. Their expense may prevent regular daily feeding, but, as a once a week treat these foods will serve your fish well. In addition to the live worm foods, you can also offer your fish some live brine shrimp. If you're so inclined you can even go about raising your own brine shrimp to feed your fish. In doing this you can offer them more nutritious treats, and more often.

FREQUENCY OF FEEDING
This can be a topic of great conjecture. How much and how often do you feed your fish? Some folks feed their fish once a day. Some people who are home most of the day feed their fish smaller amounts 4 or 5 times a day. Me, I feed 'em twice a day. No matter

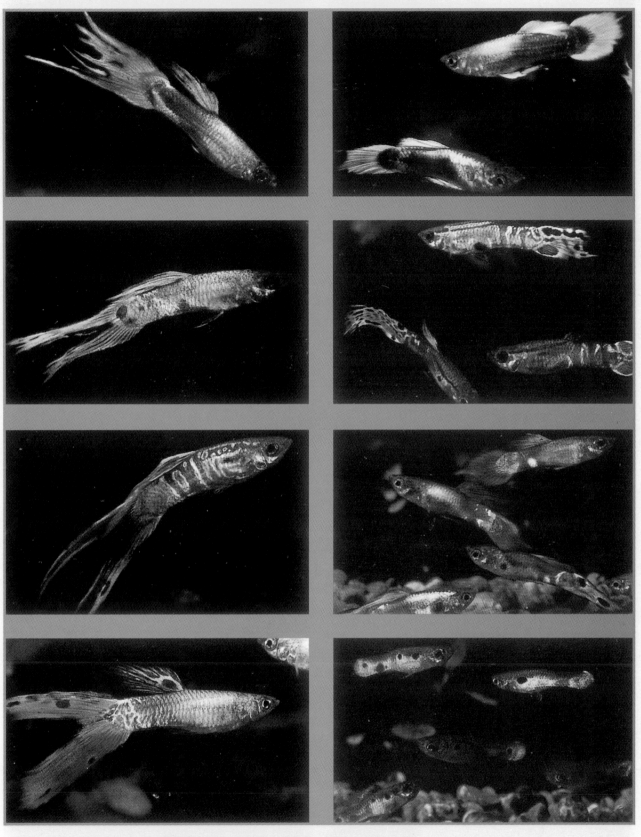

The photo in the lower right hand corner is of wild guppies. They were the original stock used to produce many more fanciful color varieties such as those shown in the other seven photos. You can see that each of the fancy guppies still carries some markings of the original wild strain. Photos and guppies by Tanaka.

which methodology you choose, keep this credo in mind. *"'Tis better to underfeed than overfeed."* There are some people who believe if a little is good, a lot is better when it comes to food. Nothing can be further from the truth when it comes to feeding your fishes. Whatever you feed them, try to see that it's all gone in 3 minutes or so. Otherwise, you may end up with a tankful of rotting food. This can wreak havoc on your filtration system. It can also lead to a sudden rise in the ammonia level of your tank.

There is never as much food available in nature as there is in your home aquarium. Therefore, fish are always on the scavenge for food. They always look and act hungry. They should. They don't know any better. Keep them foraging. To go one step further, I fast my fish once a week. Is this cruel? Nah. Normally a fasting day will send the fish into nooks and crannies of the aquarium to search out that little morsel left behind the day before. The dual function here leaves the fish to do a little housekeeping themselves.

I find that the best way to control food intake as well as monitor their nutritional requirements is to feed twice a day. In the mornings, when I'm in a hurry to get to work, I feed flakes. When I get home (after I eat) I proceed to feed the fish either a freeze-dried food or one of the frozen varieties.

When I have live foods available (which isn't always) I feed them a little more liberally and more often in order to use them up prior to spoilage. I don't care what anyone says, there is no fouler odor than a bowl of fouled, dead blackworms. Yecch!

All in all, feeding should not be a major problem, just a factor you need to give a little more consideration to than perhaps you originally thought. Variety is the key. A varied diet goes a long way toward ensuring a nutritionally complete diet.

Fancy guppies showing basically wild guppy colors. Photos and fishes by Tanaka.

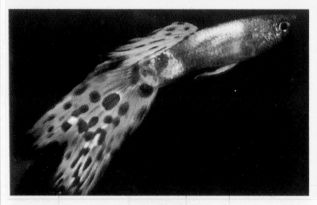

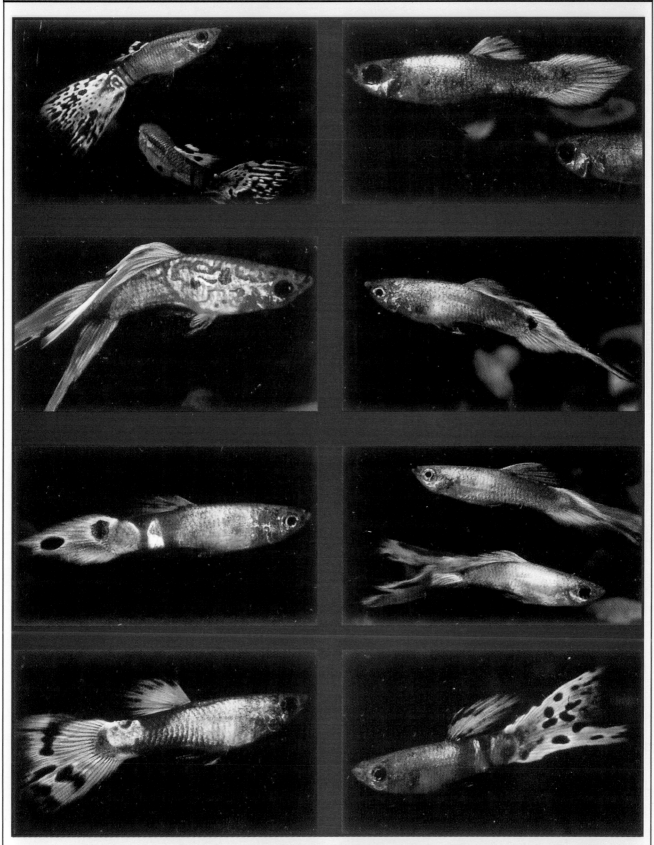

Fancy wild types from the same general strain of Tanaka guppies. There are no body patterns recognizable, only wild type variations. Photos by Tanaka.

BREEDING YOUR GUPPIES

Aside from their pretty colors, one of the first things that attracts would-be guppy keepers is the ease in which they produce offspring. Guppies are livebearers. This may be obvious to some, but many people have no idea that any fish are livebearers until they enter the hobby.

Simply speaking, fertilization take place internally and when the fry come to term they are born alive and free-swimming. Unlike most mammals, and sharks for that matter, guppies will eat their young if they do not have a place to hide or are removed from the aquarium. Other popular tropical fish that are livebearers include: mollies, swordtails, platies and other species including the North American mosquito fish.

Breeding guppies is not a difficult endeavor. Producing and fixing a strain is. "Fixing" is the process by which a majority of the offspring will mimic the gene structure of the parents on a frequently consistent basis. If you have a gorgeous green cobra guppy that you want to breed, you are going to want to find a female with a similar gene pool to bring out more gorgeous green

In one end, out the other. The mother guppy may (and usually does) go after her newborns and eat them. Photo by Hans Joachim Richter.

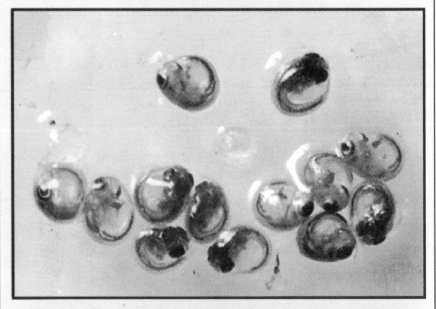

Guppy embryos extracted from the body of a dead female guppy. The eggs develop internally in the female guppy and the fry are free swimming and on their own as soon as they are born. Photo by Arend van den Nieuwenhuizen.

The three photos on the top showing males are all Tanaka's white tail strain. The remaining photos show the females of different strains. When crossed with their own children, these females produce almost uniform fry. Photo by Tanaka.

Phallichthys amates is a livebearing fish, similar to the guppy. But it is larger and the male has a more conspicuous gonopodium (the modified anal fin used to impregnate females). So we will use this as our model for sex acts in guppies. The male swims alongside the female, head to head, then he swings his gonopodium forward and inserts it into the anal pore of the female, at the same time shooting sperm packets (spermatophores) into and around her genital pore. Photos by Hans Joachim Richter.

cobra guppies. Then again, either sex could have recessive traits (traits one individual or the other does not show, but passes on) that will show up in the progeny. This is one of those difficult hurdles to overcome in an effort to produce the optimal guppy for you.

This chapter by no means will attempt to turn you into a genealogist, or even a master guppy breeder for that matter. Rather, I tend to give you a fairly comprehensive overview and let you take it from there.

The easiest way to breed your guppies is to put a male guppy in the same tank with a female guppy and let nature take its course. If you haven't figured it out already it is quite simple to distinguish a male guppy from a female. It is the males who have the long beautiful flashy tails. The females' tails are much smaller than those of their male counterparts. To add insult to injury, the ladies are often drab in comparison to the overall coloration of the males. For this reason, you will see guppies usually sold in pairs only. Otherwise, a store owner will find himself with an overabundance of females. Believe it or not many hobbyists will purchase their guppies solely for their beauty with no intention or care for breeding them.

An interesting tidbit with regard to the propagation of guppies is the female's ability to store sperm. That's right. One breeding can lead to several subsequent birthings without the male ever coming into contact after that first time. This is why it is so important to have virgin female guppies upon embarking on a serious breeding program.

How does one go about getting virgin guppies? There's no way you can be assured of spotting a virgin in a tank swarming with miscellaneous guppies in an aquarium store. There are two avenues you can follow. 1. Obtain specimens from a seller who can confidently assure you, you're getting what you pay for. Or 2. Obtain your own virgin stock by breeding purchased guppies and separating the females from the males before the males can impregnate the females.

It is difficult, but not

A tank filled with fancy guppies at the Aquarama in Singapore, about early 1990's. Photo by Dr. Herbert R. Axelrod.

impossible to distinguish the males from the females when the guppies are very young. The coloration and tail size and developing gonopodia of the males and gravid spots on the females are not obviously discernible, except to the experienced eye. You just have to keep observing the young guppies and pulling out those that show sexual characteristics. With practice (and luck) you'll be left with a pool of virgin females.

While raising your virgin females you want to be sure to put them on a good feeding program. Nutritious feedings that include as much live food as possible will ensure that your females mature into strong individuals. Equally important is the fact that hearty, healthy females will carry healthier as well as more numerous offspring. A fish lacking in nutrition will throw small yields as well as present the possibility of producing small, weak, even deformed fry.

THE ACT

When you decide your female is ready, it is time to put the father-to-be in with her. A guppy will reach its adult size in approximately six months, although it will reach sexual maturity in less than two. Putting them into a breeding program at 3 to 4 months would be a reasonable time frame to get things going.

A mature male is evidenced by his sexual organ referred to as a *gonopodium.* This organ is easily recognizable, and would pass as an unpaired fin to those uninitiated. It is a rod-like structure that emanates from the lower abdomen and tapers down to a point as it lies under to the body. As with mammals, the male will employ this organ to transfer sperm to the female through her *genital pore,* thus internally fertilizing the female.

At the Aquarama Fish Show in Singapore, Gan Aquarium Fish Farm showed samples of their guppy production.

Female guppy delivering her live babies. They can come out head first or tail first. They drop an inch or two and then swim off. Photos by Ruda Zukal.

Two greeen guppies. Some people might call them black guppies. Note the males have the modified anal fins which swing 180° forward to deliver their sperm packets. Photo by Gan Aquarium Fish Farm.

Prior to the act of fertilization the male and female guppy go through a courtship ritual prior to the ultimate act of copulation. When the male decides that it is time to do his thing, he will begin pursuit of the female throughout the aquarium, at times relentlessly. After an indeterminate number of chases he will try to corner her nose to nose. It is at this point he will start what looks like "showing off "

He will proceed to swim around her, rather than chasing her, turning every which way. He will continue this ceremony until he is assured he has the attention of the female. His goal at this point is to get her to follow him. If she does...he will continue his showing off. He will spread his fins to the point where they look as if they're going to split. Additionally he can and will intensify his coloration to further attract the female to him. Maybe us guys can learn something from these guppies. When he is sure he has her attention he will position himself in such a way so that he can manipulate his gonopodium so as to make contact with the female's genital pore.

The gonopodium has several barb-like spurs that will ensure that fertilization can occur without the female slipping away. This courtship ritual can go on for several hours. The male will make a number of tries at this so that a successful insemination is insured. While attempts may exceed 100, it is likely that less than 10% are successsful. It is a good idea to remove the male after 2 hours or so. If not, he will continue his pursuit, thus exhausting the female.

Remember, the female will now be storing these little sperm packets to use not only now, but at a later date. For this reason it is important that you keep track of the male used in order to successfully chart your breeding program. If you put a different male in with the same female, if she has not used up the stored sperm from the first breeding (3 or 4 successive broods) it will be difficult to know who has fathered what.

Gestation can last from 4 to six weeks. There are several factors determining this, including conditions such as light, temperature, food, and the overall condition of the mother guppy. It is best to get a pregnant female into a tank of her own no more than halfway through the gestation period. Netting or handling a pregnant guppy could cause premature delivery and certain mortality to the resulting fry.

A healthy mother guppy can deliver as few as 20 or as many as 100 fry. There are accounts of them producing more and your mileage may vary. While in the carrying stage you still want to feed the mother as varied and nutritious a diet as possible. Keep in mind, she could be eating for 101!

RAISING THE BABIES

Raising baby guppies into full-fledged beautiful adult guppies is an art or science in itself and is not nearly as easy as it may seem. Those fish breeders working with egglayers will tell you that the hard part is not getting the fish to spawn and lay eggs, but rather in the rearing of the subsequent fry. The same holds true for livebearing guppies.

As always, Nature has its way of ensuring the survival of a species. With fish, it's a numbers game. Many fish will throw hundreds of eggs, of which only a handful may survive due to predation and other natural causes. This is, of course, survival of the

fittest. Livebearers, such as guppies, can bear over one hundred young at a time, and start the whole thing over in 30 days.

Without natural predation, guppies in your aquarium will survive in much greater numbers, provided that you remove the mother once the birthing process is completed. Yes, mamma guppy will cannibalize the young as her maternal instincts fade with birth. The trick to raising them is twofold; culling and feeding.

Without upsetting too many of you culling is the process where less than acceptable specimens are destroyed. There are a number of ways to handle

Gan Aquarium Fish Farm produced this yellow snakeskin guppy strain.

The ideal guppy aquarium! The beautiful, dense vegetation serves many purposes. The two most important purposes are a place to hide for the pregnant female and a place to hide for the fry. Photo by Arend van den Nieuwenhuizen.

In Czechoslovakia in 1970, these were considered fancy guppies. Today they are economically worthless. Photo by Ruda Zukal.

the process of culling. Though many won't admit it, many undesirable guppies find their way into the family toilet. Another alternative, though perhaps just as unpleasant, would be to use the culled specimens as feeder fish to some of your other tropicals.

What may seem like a more humane method is freezing them. Place the fish in a plastic bag, and place it in the freezer. Their metabolism will slow down to the point where they quickly lose consciousness followed by death. There is no pain involved with this method.

Wait a minute. Wasn't this chapter supposed to be about raising the guppies, rather than wasting them?

True, but in order to raise healthy guppies they need to be fed properly. Too much competition for available food will lead to

the ultimate demise of the weaker specimens anyway. Too much food offered into the tank will cause fouling and endanger the lives of even the most healthy individuals. A choice must be made.

The best food to feed newly born guppy babies would be brine shrimp nauplii, also known as baby brine shrimp.

This should be the staple food for your baby guppies for at least the first 4 weeks. You can combine it with some crushed flake food as a supplement to their diet. Subsequent to the one month plateau you can take a break from the baby brine shrimp routine, although continuing them on this diet would only enhance their development. Perhaps a suitable alternative would be to cut down on the live feedings if they are becoming too arduous and supplement

them with the frozen variety of brine shrimp. In addition to the brine shrimp, offerings of beefheart and bloodworms would also be beneficial.

As always, variety is the key ingredient to healthy guppies.

BRINE SHRIMP

Successfully rearing brine shrimp, as you see, is often the key to raising strong, healthy, sturdy guppies to adulthood. As previously mentioned, getting the fish to breed is the easy part. Raising the tiny progeny is where the difficulty can lie. This is why it is so important to be able to raise brine shrimp successfully. It's not that it's so hard, but as with any new venture, practice makes perfect. The directions for hatching the brine shrimp sound simple enough, but what actually happens after trying to raise several batches unsuccessfully is another.

Marine shrimp (Artemia salina) now harvested domestically for the aquarium trade are one of the most nutritious and easy to prepare foods for baby guppies or other baby fish for that matter. The eggs of the shrimp are dried and packaged for sale. They are simple to hatch out if you follow several simple steps. The general principles of hatching are easily followed by referring to the instructions on the package. Quite simply, you want to add the eggs to water with the appropriate amount of salt (non-iodized) added, and within 24 to 48 hours they will hatch.

Hatching and hatchery designs vary from hobbyist to hobbyist, though at the outset the simplest design will suit your needs. I built a simple box with one open side. On the top of the box I made a hole with a 4 inch diameter. Atop the box I sat a 1/2 gallon plastic juice container with the narrow neck cut off. Inside the box I sat an incandescent light fixture with a 100 watt bulb. This is the essence of my simple yet effective brine shrimp hatching contraption. Here's how you put it into effect.

I add the appropriate amount of salt to the tap water. I run an airstone into the water until all of the salt dissolves. Once the salt has dissolved I add the appropriate amount of

brine shrimp eggs to the volume of water. Don't try to exceed what the instructions say thinking you'll hatch more. You'll just end up with a mess.

Keep the eggs aerated by leaving the airstone in the bottle. After 24 hours or so, you can check to see if you have a hatch. You can almost guarantee a 24 hour hatch if you put a heater in the bottle (not if it's plastic, though) and get the temperature up to 80 degrees F. Otherwise, you should have your brine shrimp hatch in no more than 48 hours.

To check on your hatch's progress, remove the airstone and let things settle. At this point turn on the light. Have it directed right at the hole in the box which you have your bottle situated atop. The hatched brine shrimp will begin to congregate toward the light source. If you look closely,

you should see a quivering orange mass moving about toward the bottom of the bottle. Additionally you will see the brownish egg casings floating at the top. The trick is to remove the shrimp without the egg casings.

I have found the simplest way of removing the brine shrimp is by means of siphoning. I use the standard 3/8" flexible airline tubing as my siphon. Of course, you have to use a little mouth action to get the siphon going. The uninitiated will get a little (maybe a gulp) salt water in their mouths. Of course, with a little practice you can avoid this malady altogether.

Let the siphon empty into a brine shrimp net. This is usually a little 3" net found at your local aquarium shop with very close-knit meshing in order to prevent the very little brine shrimp from going right through. With your hand guide the airline tubing around where you can see the shrimp congregating. This whole process may take 30 seconds. At this point cease siphoning. Let the net drain of water. What you should see if you've performed this task correctly is a dollop of brine shrimp. Rinse them in a little fresh water while they're still in the net, then dole them out to your guppy babies. You will see them gulp them down with fervor. Once batch #1 has hatched and you begin

A mosquito larva, with breathing apparatus at water surface. Whether alive or in frozen or freeze-dried state, mosquito larvae are an excellent food for guppies. Photo by R. Schreiber.

Not all fancy strains are true strains. Many times guppy tanks are filled with male guppies, no two of which are alike. These are not strains. To demonstrate a strain, a breeder must produce at least 10 almost identical fish from the same female/male breeding. Photos by Tanaka.

A champion male double swordtail guppy. Bred and photographed by Tanaka.

using it, it's time to start batch #2 in a separate bottle. Each batch will last from 2 to 3 days depending on how much you're feeding. This is why you always want to have a subsequent batch brewing.

If you do run out of brine shrimp, or you just have a dud batch (this can happen) you can substitute finely ground flake food in the interim. Alternatively, you could also grind some frozen adult brine shrimp through a strainer as a suitable substitute. But do get back to the live baby brine as soon as possible.

One final note of importance. Upon siphoning out your baby brine, if you notice the coloration is brown, not orange, *do not* feed to your guppies. The brown color is indicative of the egg casings. The fish will eat these, but in most instances they will bind in the small fish's digestive tract, causing constipation and death. If this happens, try mixing up the contents of the jar, let things settle with the light on, and try again. If still unsuccessful, discard that batch and start anew.

You've just been given a nice serving of information regarding guppies. To some of you it may be a bit much to digest. I can almost hear some of you saying, "I had no idea so much was involved. All I wanted to do was keep a few guppies and have some babies." There are some practitioners in the hobby who may actually tell you that if you're not going to be serious about what you're doing, you shouldn't be doing it at all.

What I say to you, the reader, the hobbyist, the average Joe, is that there is room in the hobby for every degree of expertise as well as commitment. You don't have to take breeding guppies totally seriously to derive pleasure and enjoyment. If you want to throw a male and a female together and see what happens, go for it. Have fun. Not only will you have fun, but if children are

Magnificent double swordtail guppies bred by Tanaka. They have unusually long swords. Photo by Tanaka.

Scarftail guppies featuring the eye-spot on the belly. Photo and fish by Tanaka.

I.F.G.A.

The International Fancy Guppy Association is composed of regional splinter groups throughout the United States and abroad committed to the hobby (or even profession) of guppy keeping. These various groups will sponsor I.F.G.A. sanctioned events where ardent guppy keepers show their fish for trophies, prizes, and titles. You will find serious enthusiasts as well as novices looking to learn a thing or two.

There are 10 I.F.G.A. sponsored shows a year in various locales, hosted by individual guppy clubs. Of those 10 shows, one is labelled as the show of shows. The last one (1996) was held in Florida with over 500 entries. Guppy breeders either attend these shows personally, or send their fish by mail to be judged.

In addition to sponsoring these shows, the I.F.G.A. puts out a monthly newsletter titled *The Bulletin.* This publication informs its members of upcoming shows, news of new guppy strains being introduced, as well as informed articles by experts on the rearing of guppies. Additionally, if you're really looking for that hard to find guppy and don't want to be duped, this is a great means to find a true breeder of a strain.

involved it is also an exiting experience for them as well.

I wouldn't be too surprised, however, if you went the next step further and tried to breed green cobras, or half-blacks, or any other strain for that matter. It does become a fixation, and is habit forming. So much so that an internationally recognized organization exists to specifically promote the keeping, breeding and showing of guppies. This association is known as the International Fancy Guppy Association, IFGA for short.

Not all Tanaka strains are commercial successes. The fish shown on this plate are mixed successes. The top two photos are fish which could be sold in quantity but only at a low price. The other six fish had to be sold at prices lower than the cost of their feeding! Photo by Tanaka.

In 1986 this male took BEST IN
SHOW at a German guppy contest.
Photo by Hans Joachim Richter.

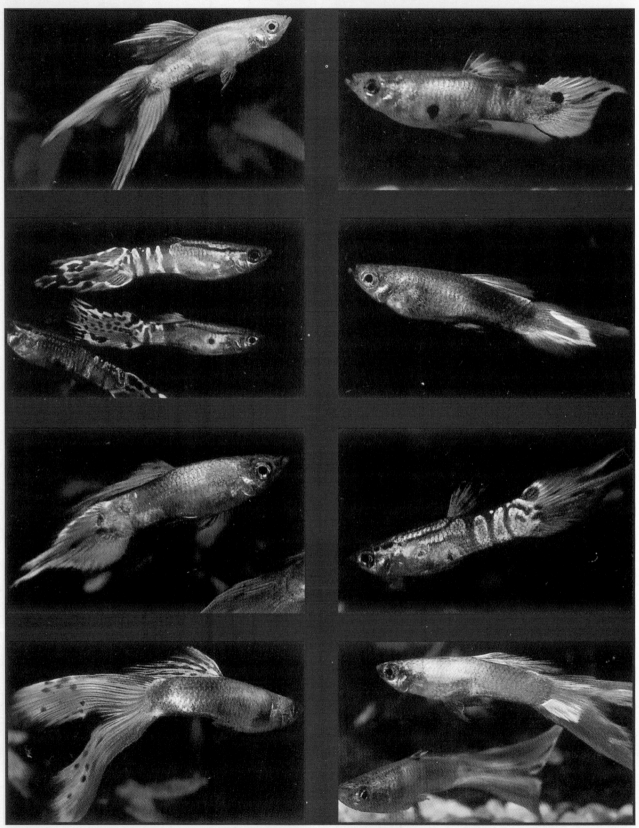

Modern Japanese guppies are judged by their tails. Both the shape and color of the tails must be interesting. Here are some of Tanaka's suggestions. Photos by Tanaka.

DISEASES

Just as there is nothing more spectacular than a tank full of healthy vibrant colorful guppies, conversely nothing can be as bleak and dreary as a tank full of diseased fish. Of course, at the outset disease is probably the last thing you want to think about as you prepare your aquarium for fish. Unfortunately, especially for beginners, disease can be inevitable.

How does it happen? How can you cure it? How can you prevent it from happening again? In this chapter we will answer all of these questions in layman's terms. This chapter will not act as a symposium on fish physiology and parasitology, but rather a synopsis on controlling, and more preferably avoiding, disease in your aquarium.

ICHTHYOPHTHIRIUS

Let's call the most common aquarium disease, caused by the protozoan parasite *Ichthyophthirius multifiliis*, ich (pronounced ick) for short. Another name for this oft encountered malady would be white spot disease. I can tell you right now, if you go back to the section on water quality and read what I wrote about salt in the aquarium and use it, you can almost eliminate the

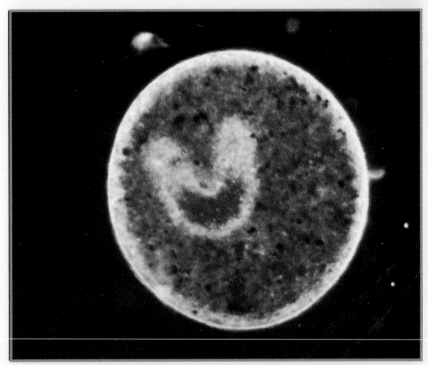

If you took one of the white spots from a guppy, it would look like this when enlarged. This is an *Ichthyophthirius* cyst (fertilized egg). Photo by Frickhinger.

This is a black neon, *Hyphessobrycon herbertaxelrodi*, showing the white spots characteristic of an *Ichthyophthirius* (ich) infection. Photo by Dieter Untergasser.

outbreak of ich.

Inasmuch as it is the disease most frequently seen on fish we'll deal with ich in the most detail. There are several ways fish can contract ich. These are the most common.

1. Introducing it into your aquarium by way of other fish.

2. Stress induced by various factors.

The presence of ich is characterized by little white spots (like sprinkled salt) that appear about the fish's body. The fish can start out with several spots scattered or conglomerated about the fish. Ich, untreated, will quickly spread over the fish's entire body. It is not a pretty sight, and you can rest assured your fish is not too happy either.

When purchasing guppies, inspect the tank they are in. If there is the slightest presence of ich, don't buy any fish from that tank...not even those that appear healthy. Odds are they are harboring the parasite and it has not become visible to the eye yet. This is how ich can be transmitted to an otherwise healthy aquarium.

As humans have a natural immunity system built into their anatomies, so, too, do fishes. Their immune systems consist of a mucus-like covering about their bodies. This is referred to as a *slime coat.* When a fish is subject to physiological or environmental stress, this coating can dissipate. When the slime coat does this, it leaves the fish wide open for an array of ever-present organisms to attack. This would include ich. Fortunately, there are cures for ich, both natural and medicinal. I prefer to apply the natural method myself, as medicines can deplete your *Nitrosomonas* and *Nitrobacter* bacteria (there's those words again!) if you overdo it. The first thing you want to examine is why

This is a golden Mickey Mouse highfin platy female showing the ich infection. We are using larger fishes to illustrate ich because ich is very difficult to see on guppies. Photo by Dr. Herbert R. Axelrod.

At the guppy show in Leipzig, Germany, three types of swordtail guppies were on display. The upper, lower and double swordtails are shown from top to bottom. Photo by Hans Joachim Richter.

your fish came down with ich in the first place. Ask yourself these questions: Is there an ammonia build-up in the tank? Are there fish in the tank chasing down the guppies causing stress? Is the pH out of whack? Is the tank due for a water change? Is the temperature of the tank too low? If the answer to any of these questions is *yes*, take the proper steps to correct the situation.

Natural method: Do a 33% water change. Next, gradually raise the tank temperature to the high 80's F. Suspend feeding at this point as well. Keep the temperature at this level for the next 48 hours. The high temperature will speed up the life cycle of the ich parasite, and the parasites

will drop off. If within 48 hours the fish do not appear to be free of the white spots, go for another 24 hours. After that you'll want to go the medicinal route. Stay tuned. If they are gone perform another 33% water change. Gradually let the temperature drop down to normal (72 to 76 degrees Fahrenheit). At this point I highly recommend a dose of a slime coat regenerator containing aloe. This works wonders for the fish in promoting a regeneration of their slime coat.

AND DON'T FORGET THE SALT. IF IT ISN'T ALREADY IN THERE, GET IT IN.

Since I learned about adding salt to the aquarium some ten years ago, I have

never had a case of ich.

The medicinal approach:

There are a number of ich medications out there under various trade names that can be effective in eliminating this pesky parasite. Be sure to follow the directions carefully, and don't over or under-medicate. It is important to make a water change prior to and subsequent to treatment. Additionally, make sure to remove any carbon from your filtration system while medicating. The active ingredients in the medication can be rendered inert by the carbon as they pass through it. Replace your carbon once you have ceased medicating the tank. It wouldn't hurt to raise the

An easily recognizable disease is abdominal dropsy characterized by the raised scales and the distended eyes. Photo by Dieter Untergasser.

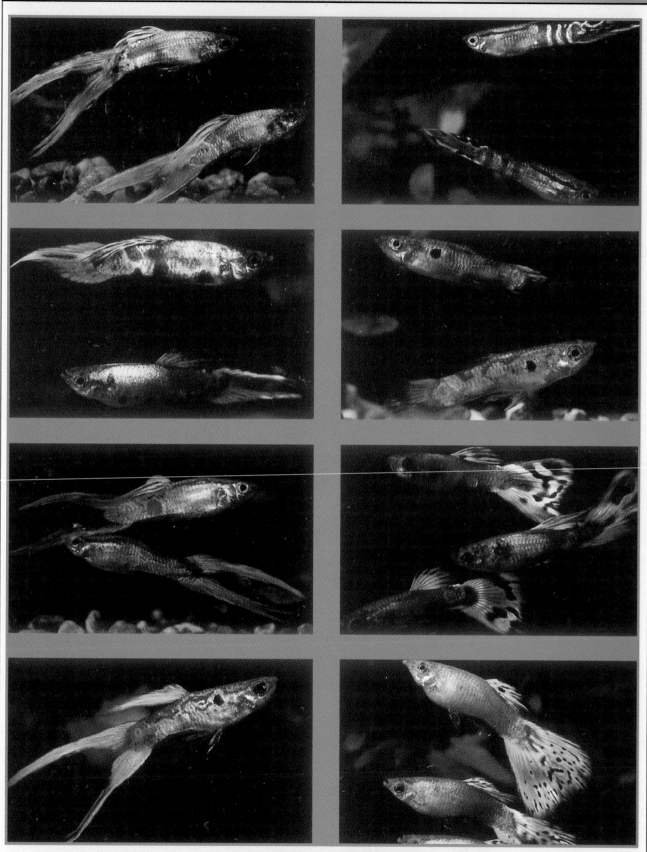

Tanaka's Japanese guppy types based upon original wild strains. Photos by Tanaka.

temperature of the tank simultaneously (slowly, that is) while medicating.

After medicating with an ich remedy, you should follow your treatment up with a dose of nitrofurazone to aid in the healing of the wounds left by the ich parasite. Some commercial products for ich cure contain nitrofurazone as well. A good dose of an aloe based slime coat regenerating product will help the fish regenerate its slime coat to reduce any further infection.

FUNGUS

Fungus is usually the second most common affliction to affect your fish. Fungus is, once again, usually derived from poor water quality and/or stress related stimuli within the aquarium.

Fungus is mostly characterized by cottony tufts about the mouth or tail region. Coloration ranges from white to gray. Needless to say, this is as unpleasant to look at as it is for the fish to suffer with. Inasmuch as there are over 50,000 species of fungus, let us limit our discussion to the most common to affect your fish, *Saprolegnia.*

This fungus will most often show its ugly face when there is decay occurring within the aquaria. If you've ever found a dead fish covered in a ghostly cloud, that is fungus. The same thing can occur when there is

decaying uneaten food within the tank. But how does it get to those fish that are swimming around. It's that old "stress-word" again.

If your fish are stressed due to poor water conditions, and that defense system of theirs breaks down, it's an opening for Mr. Fungus to attack and attach to wounded areas on the fish. Unfortunately, fungus is not as easily removable by natural methods as is ich. There are, however, a number of fungus remedies on the market that will do a decent job of eradicating the sucker. But first, do that water change. Again, if you haven't already, add that salt. Now medicate. (Don't forget to remove the carbon.) Suspend feeding for the 48 hours while you're medicating, and do another water change subsequent to your last dose.

FIN ROT

If you are keeping your guppies with other species of fishes, I wouldn't be too surprised to see them afflicted with this ailment. While fin rot (also referred to as tail rot in guppies) can be brought on by various bacteria or poor water conditions, the root of this evil most likely is brought on by tail nipping.

Aside from visual observation, a guppy afflicted with fin rot will display characteristics including: split and ragged fins, and stumpy or missing fins, all possibly exhibiting

subsequent fungal growth. The good news is the fins will regenerate with swift attention to the affliction.

First things first. If you have any "public enemies" in your aquarium guilty of fin nipping, get them out. Otherwise, remove the guppies. It won't make any sense to treat the symptoms without removing the problem. Perform a one-third water change and treat the tank with one of the available tetracycline medications. Remember these two things again. 1. If you don't have salt in your aquarium...add it! 2. Remove any carbon filtration while medicating.

If you are treating a resultant fungal infection you can begin medicating for fungus first, followed the next day with co-incidental treatment for the fin rot. Make sure you make a one-third water change subsequent to all treatments.

GUPPY DISEASE

This is an infirmity with symptoms very similar to ich, but it is caused by a protozoan named *Tetrahymena.* What does all this mean for your guppies?

Like ich, there are white spots that will appear about the fish's body. In conjunction with the spots you probably will see the sloughing off of skin along with pertruding scales. Finally, you will notice erratic or very poor swimming on the part of your fish.

Examples of fancy deltatail guppies based mainly on Singapore types.

One of Tanaka's Fancy strains included these remarkably similar males. Photo by Tanaka.

Most often, guppies will arrive at your local retailer harboring the disease. It usually perpetuates itself through poor nutrition, poor water quality, or decaying organic matter in their holding facility. This is why it's so important for you to inspect your purchases as thoroughly as possible before bringing them home. Don't be so quick to assassinate your dealer, however. They can't control everything. When you do business with a dealer who offers you healthy fish for the most part, it is a good idea to stick with him. More than likely he has developed relationships with distributors with whom he is confident, and who have given him quality shipments over a protracted period of time.

Unlike ich, the *Tetrahymena* protozoan is more stubborn and difficult to eradicate than the white spot. Its nature is to embed itself into the musculature of the guppy or even enter the bloodstream. Treat in the same way you would for ich. Keep in mind, however that this is a little bit tougher to get rid of, so it may require more than one treatment.